# DISC GOLF

Date:

Course:

| Par: | Distance: |
|---|---|
| Weather: | Wind: |

| Hole | 1 | 2 | 3 | 4 | 5 | 6 | 7 | 8 | 9 | Out |
|---|---|---|---|---|---|---|---|---|---|---|
| Par | | | | | | | | | | |
| Distance | | | | | | | | | | |
| | | | | | | | | | | |
| | | | | | | | | | | |
| | | | | | | | | | | |
| | | | | | | | | | | |

| Hole | 10 | 11 | 12 | 13 | 14 | 15 | 16 | 17 | 18 | In | Total |
|---|---|---|---|---|---|---|---|---|---|---|---|
| Par | | | | | | | | | | | |
| Distance | | | | | | | | | | | |
| | | | | | | | | | | | |
| | | | | | | | | | | | |
| | | | | | | | | | | | |
| | | | | | | | | | | | |

Notes: _____

_____

_____

_____

_____

# DISC GOLF SCORECARD

| Date: | | Time: | |
|---|---|---|---|
| Course: | | | |
| Par: | | Distance: | |
| Weather: | | Wind: | |

| Hole | 1 | 2 | 3 | 4 | 5 | 6 | 7 | 8 | 9 | Out |
|---|---|---|---|---|---|---|---|---|---|---|
| Par | | | | | | | | | | |
| Distance | | | | | | | | | | |
| | | | | | | | | | | |
| | | | | | | | | | | |
| | | | | | | | | | | |
| | | | | | | | | | | |

| Hole | 10 | 11 | 12 | 13 | 14 | 15 | 16 | 17 | 18 | In | Total |
|---|---|---|---|---|---|---|---|---|---|---|---|
| Par | | | | | | | | | | | |
| Distance | | | | | | | | | | | |
| | | | | | | | | | | | |
| | | | | | | | | | | | |
| | | | | | | | | | | | |
| | | | | | | | | | | | |

Notes: _____

_____

_____

_____

_____

# DISC GOLF SCORECARD

| Date: | | Time: | |
|---|---|---|---|
| Course: | | | |
| Par: | | Distance: | |
| Weather: | | Wind: | |

| Hole | 1 | 2 | 3 | 4 | 5 | 6 | 7 | 8 | 9 | Out |
|---|---|---|---|---|---|---|---|---|---|---|
| Par | | | | | | | | | | |
| Distance | | | | | | | | | | |
| | | | | | | | | | | |
| | | | | | | | | | | |
| | | | | | | | | | | |
| | | | | | | | | | | |

| Hole | 10 | 11 | 12 | 13 | 14 | 15 | 16 | 17 | 18 | In | Total |
|---|---|---|---|---|---|---|---|---|---|---|---|
| Par | | | | | | | | | | | |
| Distance | | | | | | | | | | | |
| | | | | | | | | | | | |
| | | | | | | | | | | | |
| | | | | | | | | | | | |
| | | | | | | | | | | | |

Notes: _____

_____

_____

_____

_____

# DISC GOLF SCORECARD

| Date: | | Time: | |
|-------|--|-------|--|
| Course: | | | |
| Par: | | Distance: | |
| Weather: | | Wind: | |

| Hole | 1 | 2 | 3 | 4 | 5 | 6 | 7 | 8 | 9 | Out |
|------|---|---|---|---|---|---|---|---|---|-----|
| Par | | | | | | | | | | |
| Distance | | | | | | | | | | |
| | | | | | | | | | | |
| | | | | | | | | | | |
| | | | | | | | | | | |
| | | | | | | | | | | |

| Hole | 10 | 11 | 12 | 13 | 14 | 15 | 16 | 17 | 18 | In | Total |
|------|----|----|----|----|----|----|----|----|----|----|-------|
| Par | | | | | | | | | | | |
| Distance | | | | | | | | | | | |
| | | | | | | | | | | | |
| | | | | | | | | | | | |
| | | | | | | | | | | | |
| | | | | | | | | | | | |

Notes: _____

_____

_____

_____

_____

# DISC GOLF SCORECARD

| Date: | | Time: |
|---|---|---|
| Course: | | |
| Par: | | Distance: |
| Weather: | | Wind: |

| Hole | 1 | 2 | 3 | 4 | 5 | 6 | 7 | 8 | 9 | Out |
|---|---|---|---|---|---|---|---|---|---|---|
| Par | | | | | | | | | | |
| Distance | | | | | | | | | | |
| | | | | | | | | | | |
| | | | | | | | | | | |
| | | | | | | | | | | |
| | | | | | | | | | | |

| Hole | 10 | 11 | 12 | 13 | 14 | 15 | 16 | 17 | 18 | In | Total |
|---|---|---|---|---|---|---|---|---|---|---|---|
| Par | | | | | | | | | | | |
| Distance | | | | | | | | | | | |
| | | | | | | | | | | | |
| | | | | | | | | | | | |
| | | | | | | | | | | | |
| | | | | | | | | | | | |

Notes: _____
_____
_____
_____
_____

# DISC GOLF SCORECARD

| Date: | | Time: | |
|---|---|---|---|
| Course: | | | |
| Par: | | Distance: | |
| Weather: | | Wind: | |

| Hole | 1 | 2 | 3 | 4 | 5 | 6 | 7 | 8 | 9 | Out |
|---|---|---|---|---|---|---|---|---|---|---|
| Par | | | | | | | | | | |
| Distance | | | | | | | | | | |
| | | | | | | | | | | |
| | | | | | | | | | | |
| | | | | | | | | | | |
| | | | | | | | | | | |

| Hole | 10 | 11 | 12 | 13 | 14 | 15 | 16 | 17 | 18 | In | Total |
|---|---|---|---|---|---|---|---|---|---|---|---|
| Par | | | | | | | | | | | |
| Distance | | | | | | | | | | | |
| | | | | | | | | | | | |
| | | | | | | | | | | | |
| | | | | | | | | | | | |
| | | | | | | | | | | | |

Notes: _____
_____
_____
_____
_____

# DISC GOLF SCORECARD

| Date: | Time: |
|---|---|
| Course: | |
| Par: | Distance: |
| Weather: | Wind: |

| Hole | 1 | 2 | 3 | 4 | 5 | 6 | 7 | 8 | 9 | Out |
|---|---|---|---|---|---|---|---|---|---|---|
| Par | | | | | | | | | | |
| Distance | | | | | | | | | | |
| | | | | | | | | | | |
| | | | | | | | | | | |
| | | | | | | | | | | |
| | | | | | | | | | | |

| Hole | 10 | 11 | 12 | 13 | 14 | 15 | 16 | 17 | 18 | In | Total |
|---|---|---|---|---|---|---|---|---|---|---|---|
| Par | | | | | | | | | | | |
| Distance | | | | | | | | | | | |
| | | | | | | | | | | | |
| | | | | | | | | | | | |
| | | | | | | | | | | | |
| | | | | | | | | | | | |

Notes: _____
_____
_____
_____
_____

# DISC GOLF SCORECARD

| Date: | | Time: | |
|-------|--|-------|--|
| Course: | | | |
| Par: | | Distance: | |
| Weather: | | Wind: | |

| Hole | 1 | 2 | 3 | 4 | 5 | 6 | 7 | 8 | 9 | Out |
|------|---|---|---|---|---|---|---|---|---|-----|
| Par | | | | | | | | | | |
| Distance | | | | | | | | | | |
| | | | | | | | | | | |
| | | | | | | | | | | |
| | | | | | | | | | | |
| | | | | | | | | | | |

| Hole | 10 | 11 | 12 | 13 | 14 | 15 | 16 | 17 | 18 | In | Total |
|------|----|----|----|----|----|----|----|----|----|----|-------|
| Par | | | | | | | | | | | |
| Distance | | | | | | | | | | | |
| | | | | | | | | | | | |
| | | | | | | | | | | | |
| | | | | | | | | | | | |
| | | | | | | | | | | | |

Notes: _____

_____

_____

_____

# DISC GOLF SCORECARD

| Date: | Time: |
|---|---|
| Course: | |
| Par: | Distance: |
| Weather: | Wind: |

| Hole | 1 | 2 | 3 | 4 | 5 | 6 | 7 | 8 | 9 | Out |
|---|---|---|---|---|---|---|---|---|---|---|
| Par | | | | | | | | | | |
| Distance | | | | | | | | | | |
| | | | | | | | | | | |
| | | | | | | | | | | |
| | | | | | | | | | | |
| | | | | | | | | | | |

| Hole | 10 | 11 | 12 | 13 | 14 | 15 | 16 | 17 | 18 | In | Total |
|---|---|---|---|---|---|---|---|---|---|---|---|
| Par | | | | | | | | | | | |
| Distance | | | | | | | | | | | |
| | | | | | | | | | | | |
| | | | | | | | | | | | |
| | | | | | | | | | | | |
| | | | | | | | | | | | |

Notes: _____

_____

_____

_____

_____

# DISC GOLF SCORECARD

| Date: | | Time: | |
|---|---|---|---|
| Course: | | | |
| Par: | | Distance: | |
| Weather: | | Wind: | |

| Hole | 1 | 2 | 3 | 4 | 5 | 6 | 7 | 8 | 9 | Out |
|---|---|---|---|---|---|---|---|---|---|---|
| Par | | | | | | | | | | |
| Distance | | | | | | | | | | |
| | | | | | | | | | | |
| | | | | | | | | | | |
| | | | | | | | | | | |
| | | | | | | | | | | |

| Hole | 10 | 11 | 12 | 13 | 14 | 15 | 16 | 17 | 18 | In | Total |
|---|---|---|---|---|---|---|---|---|---|---|---|
| Par | | | | | | | | | | | |
| Distance | | | | | | | | | | | |
| | | | | | | | | | | | |
| | | | | | | | | | | | |
| | | | | | | | | | | | |
| | | | | | | | | | | | |

Notes: _____

_____

_____

_____

# DISC GOLF SCORECARD

| Date: | | Time: | |
|-------|---|-------|---|
| Course: | | | |
| Par: | | Distance: | |
| Weather: | | Wind: | |

| Hole | 1 | 2 | 3 | 4 | 5 | 6 | 7 | 8 | 9 | Out |
|----------|---|---|---|---|---|---|---|---|---|-----|
| Par | | | | | | | | | | |
| Distance | | | | | | | | | | |
| | | | | | | | | | | |
| | | | | | | | | | | |
| | | | | | | | | | | |
| | | | | | | | | | | |

| Hole | 10 | 11 | 12 | 13 | 14 | 15 | 16 | 17 | 18 | In | Total |
|----------|----|----|----|----|----|----|----|----|----|----|-------|
| Par | | | | | | | | | | | |
| Distance | | | | | | | | | | | |
| | | | | | | | | | | | |
| | | | | | | | | | | | |
| | | | | | | | | | | | |
| | | | | | | | | | | | |

Notes: _____
_____
_____
_____
_____

# DISC GOLF SCORECARD

| Date: | Time: |
|-------|-------|
| Course: | |
| Par: | Distance: |
| Weather: | Wind: |

| Hole | 1 | 2 | 3 | 4 | 5 | 6 | 7 | 8 | 9 | Out |
|------|---|---|---|---|---|---|---|---|---|-----|
| Par | | | | | | | | | | |
| Distance | | | | | | | | | | |
| | | | | | | | | | | |
| | | | | | | | | | | |
| | | | | | | | | | | |
| | | | | | | | | | | |

| Hole | 10 | 11 | 12 | 13 | 14 | 15 | 16 | 17 | 18 | In | Total |
|------|----|----|----|----|----|----|----|----|----|----|-------|
| Par | | | | | | | | | | | |
| Distance | | | | | | | | | | | |
| | | | | | | | | | | | |
| | | | | | | | | | | | |
| | | | | | | | | | | | |
| | | | | | | | | | | | |

Notes: _____

_____

_____

_____

_____

# DISC GOLF SCORECARD

| Date: | | Time: | |
|---|---|---|---|
| Course: | | | |
| Par: | | Distance: | |
| Weather: | | Wind: | |

| Hole | 1 | 2 | 3 | 4 | 5 | 6 | 7 | 8 | 9 | Out |
|---|---|---|---|---|---|---|---|---|---|---|
| Par | | | | | | | | | | |
| Distance | | | | | | | | | | |
| | | | | | | | | | | |
| | | | | | | | | | | |
| | | | | | | | | | | |
| | | | | | | | | | | |

| Hole | 10 | 11 | 12 | 13 | 14 | 15 | 16 | 17 | 18 | In | Total |
|---|---|---|---|---|---|---|---|---|---|---|---|
| Par | | | | | | | | | | | |
| Distance | | | | | | | | | | | |
| | | | | | | | | | | | |
| | | | | | | | | | | | |
| | | | | | | | | | | | |
| | | | | | | | | | | | |

Notes: _____

_____

_____

_____

_____

# DISC GOLF SCORECARD

| Date: | | Time: | |
|---|---|---|---|
| Course: | | | |
| Par: | | Distance: | |
| Weather: | | Wind: | |

| Hole | 1 | 2 | 3 | 4 | 5 | 6 | 7 | 8 | 9 | Out |
|---|---|---|---|---|---|---|---|---|---|---|
| Par | | | | | | | | | | |
| Distance | | | | | | | | | | |
| | | | | | | | | | | |
| | | | | | | | | | | |
| | | | | | | | | | | |
| | | | | | | | | | | |

| Hole | 10 | 11 | 12 | 13 | 14 | 15 | 16 | 17 | 18 | In | Total |
|---|---|---|---|---|---|---|---|---|---|---|---|
| Par | | | | | | | | | | | |
| Distance | | | | | | | | | | | |
| | | | | | | | | | | | |
| | | | | | | | | | | | |
| | | | | | | | | | | | |
| | | | | | | | | | | | |

Notes: _____
_____
_____
_____
_____

# DISC GOLF SCORECARD

| Date: | | Time: | |
|---|---|---|---|
| Course: | | | |
| Par: | | Distance: | |
| Weather: | | Wind: | |

| Hole | 1 | 2 | 3 | 4 | 5 | 6 | 7 | 8 | 9 | Out |
|---|---|---|---|---|---|---|---|---|---|---|
| Par | | | | | | | | | | |
| Distance | | | | | | | | | | |
| | | | | | | | | | | |
| | | | | | | | | | | |
| | | | | | | | | | | |
| | | | | | | | | | | |

| Hole | 10 | 11 | 12 | 13 | 14 | 15 | 16 | 17 | 18 | In | Total |
|---|---|---|---|---|---|---|---|---|---|---|---|
| Par | | | | | | | | | | | |
| Distance | | | | | | | | | | | |
| | | | | | | | | | | | |
| | | | | | | | | | | | |
| | | | | | | | | | | | |
| | | | | | | | | | | | |

Notes: _____

_____

_____

_____

_____

# DISC GOLF SCORECARD

| Date: | | Time: | |
|---|---|---|---|
| Course: | | | |
| Par: | | Distance: | |
| Weather: | | Wind: | |

| Hole | 1 | 2 | 3 | 4 | 5 | 6 | 7 | 8 | 9 | Out |
|---|---|---|---|---|---|---|---|---|---|---|
| Par | | | | | | | | | | |
| Distance | | | | | | | | | | |
| | | | | | | | | | | |
| | | | | | | | | | | |
| | | | | | | | | | | |
| | | | | | | | | | | |

| Hole | 10 | 11 | 12 | 13 | 14 | 15 | 16 | 17 | 18 | In | Total |
|---|---|---|---|---|---|---|---|---|---|---|---|
| Par | | | | | | | | | | | |
| Distance | | | | | | | | | | | |
| | | | | | | | | | | | |
| | | | | | | | | | | | |
| | | | | | | | | | | | |
| | | | | | | | | | | | |

Notes: _____

_____

_____

_____

_____

# DISC GOLF SCORECARD

| Date: | | Time: | |
|---|---|---|---|
| Course: | | | |
| Par: | | Distance: | |
| Weather: | | Wind: | |

| Hole | 1 | 2 | 3 | 4 | 5 | 6 | 7 | 8 | 9 | Out |
|---|---|---|---|---|---|---|---|---|---|---|
| Par | | | | | | | | | | |
| Distance | | | | | | | | | | |
| | | | | | | | | | | |
| | | | | | | | | | | |
| | | | | | | | | | | |
| | | | | | | | | | | |

| Hole | 10 | 11 | 12 | 13 | 14 | 15 | 16 | 17 | 18 | In | Total |
|---|---|---|---|---|---|---|---|---|---|---|---|
| Par | | | | | | | | | | | |
| Distance | | | | | | | | | | | |
| | | | | | | | | | | | |
| | | | | | | | | | | | |
| | | | | | | | | | | | |
| | | | | | | | | | | | |

Notes: _____
_____
_____
_____
_____

# DISC GOLF SCORECARD

| Date: | | Time: | |
|---|---|---|---|
| Course: | | | |
| Par: | | Distance: | |
| Weather: | | Wind: | |

| Hole | 1 | 2 | 3 | 4 | 5 | 6 | 7 | 8 | 9 | Out |
|---|---|---|---|---|---|---|---|---|---|---|
| Par | | | | | | | | | | |
| Distance | | | | | | | | | | |
| | | | | | | | | | | |
| | | | | | | | | | | |
| | | | | | | | | | | |
| | | | | | | | | | | |

| Hole | 10 | 11 | 12 | 13 | 14 | 15 | 16 | 17 | 18 | In | Total |
|---|---|---|---|---|---|---|---|---|---|---|---|
| Par | | | | | | | | | | | |
| Distance | | | | | | | | | | | |
| | | | | | | | | | | | |
| | | | | | | | | | | | |
| | | | | | | | | | | | |
| | | | | | | | | | | | |

Notes: _____

_____

_____

_____

# DISC GOLF SCORECARD

| Date: | | Time: | |
|---|---|---|---|
| Course: | | | |
| Par: | | Distance: | |
| Weather: | | Wind: | |

| Hole | 1 | 2 | 3 | 4 | 5 | 6 | 7 | 8 | 9 | Out |
|---|---|---|---|---|---|---|---|---|---|---|
| Par | | | | | | | | | | |
| Distance | | | | | | | | | | |
| | | | | | | | | | | |
| | | | | | | | | | | |
| | | | | | | | | | | |
| | | | | | | | | | | |

| Hole | 10 | 11 | 12 | 13 | 14 | 15 | 16 | 17 | 18 | In | Total |
|---|---|---|---|---|---|---|---|---|---|---|---|
| Par | | | | | | | | | | | |
| Distance | | | | | | | | | | | |
| | | | | | | | | | | | |
| | | | | | | | | | | | |
| | | | | | | | | | | | |
| | | | | | | | | | | | |

Notes: _____

_____

_____

_____

# DISC GOLF SCORECARD

| Date: | | | | | | Time: | | | |
|---|---|---|---|---|---|---|---|---|---|
| Course: | | | | | | | | | |
| Par: | | | | | | Distance: | | | |
| Weather: | | | | | | Wind: | | | |

| Hole | 1 | 2 | 3 | 4 | 5 | 6 | 7 | 8 | 9 | Out |
|---|---|---|---|---|---|---|---|---|---|---|
| Par | | | | | | | | | | |
| Distance | | | | | | | | | | |
| | | | | | | | | | | |
| | | | | | | | | | | |
| | | | | | | | | | | |
| | | | | | | | | | | |

| Hole | 10 | 11 | 12 | 13 | 14 | 15 | 16 | 17 | 18 | In | Total |
|---|---|---|---|---|---|---|---|---|---|---|---|
| Par | | | | | | | | | | | |
| Distance | | | | | | | | | | | |
| | | | | | | | | | | | |
| | | | | | | | | | | | |
| | | | | | | | | | | | |
| | | | | | | | | | | | |

Notes: _____

_____

_____

_____

_____

# DISC GOLF SCORECARD

| Date: | Time: |
|-------|-------|
| Course: | |
| Par: | Distance: |
| Weather: | Wind: |

| Hole | 1 | 2 | 3 | 4 | 5 | 6 | 7 | 8 | 9 | Out |
|------|---|---|---|---|---|---|---|---|---|-----|
| Par | | | | | | | | | | |
| Distance | | | | | | | | | | |
| | | | | | | | | | | |
| | | | | | | | | | | |
| | | | | | | | | | | |
| | | | | | | | | | | |

| Hole | 10 | 11 | 12 | 13 | 14 | 15 | 16 | 17 | 18 | In | Total |
|------|----|----|----|----|----|----|----|----|----|----|-------|
| Par | | | | | | | | | | | |
| Distance | | | | | | | | | | | |
| | | | | | | | | | | | |
| | | | | | | | | | | | |
| | | | | | | | | | | | |
| | | | | | | | | | | | |

Notes: _____
_____
_____
_____
_____

# DISC GOLF SCORECARD

| Date: | Time: |
|---|---|
| Course: | |
| Par: | Distance: |
| Weather: | Wind: |

| Hole | 1 | 2 | 3 | 4 | 5 | 6 | 7 | 8 | 9 | Out |
|---|---|---|---|---|---|---|---|---|---|---|
| Par | | | | | | | | | | |
| Distance | | | | | | | | | | |
| | | | | | | | | | | |
| | | | | | | | | | | |
| | | | | | | | | | | |
| | | | | | | | | | | |

| Hole | 10 | 11 | 12 | 13 | 14 | 15 | 16 | 17 | 18 | In | Total |
|---|---|---|---|---|---|---|---|---|---|---|---|
| Par | | | | | | | | | | | |
| Distance | | | | | | | | | | | |
| | | | | | | | | | | | |
| | | | | | | | | | | | |
| | | | | | | | | | | | |
| | | | | | | | | | | | |

Notes: _____

_____

_____

_____

# DISC GOLF SCORECARD

| Date: | | | | | Time: | | | | |
|---|---|---|---|---|---|---|---|---|---|
| Course: | | | | | | | | | |
| Par: | | | | | Distance: | | | | |
| Weather: | | | | | Wind: | | | | |

| Hole | 1 | 2 | 3 | 4 | 5 | 6 | 7 | 8 | 9 | Out |
|---|---|---|---|---|---|---|---|---|---|---|
| Par | | | | | | | | | | |
| Distance | | | | | | | | | | |
| | | | | | | | | | | |
| | | | | | | | | | | |
| | | | | | | | | | | |
| | | | | | | | | | | |

| Hole | 10 | 11 | 12 | 13 | 14 | 15 | 16 | 17 | 18 | In | Total |
|---|---|---|---|---|---|---|---|---|---|---|---|
| Par | | | | | | | | | | | |
| Distance | | | | | | | | | | | |
| | | | | | | | | | | | |
| | | | | | | | | | | | |
| | | | | | | | | | | | |
| | | | | | | | | | | | |

Notes: _____

_____

_____

_____

_____

# DISC GOLF SCORECARD

| Date: | | | | | Time: | | | | | |
|---|---|---|---|---|---|---|---|---|---|---|
| Course: | | | | | | | | | | |
| Par: | | | | | Distance: | | | | | |
| Weather: | | | | | Wind: | | | | | |

| Hole | 1 | 2 | 3 | 4 | 5 | 6 | 7 | 8 | 9 | Out |
|---|---|---|---|---|---|---|---|---|---|---|
| Par | | | | | | | | | | |
| Distance | | | | | | | | | | |
| | | | | | | | | | | |
| | | | | | | | | | | |
| | | | | | | | | | | |
| | | | | | | | | | | |

| Hole | 10 | 11 | 12 | 13 | 14 | 15 | 16 | 17 | 18 | In | Total |
|---|---|---|---|---|---|---|---|---|---|---|---|
| Par | | | | | | | | | | | |
| Distance | | | | | | | | | | | |
| | | | | | | | | | | | |
| | | | | | | | | | | | |
| | | | | | | | | | | | |
| | | | | | | | | | | | |

Notes: _____

_____

_____

_____

_____

# DISC GOLF SCORECARD

| Date: | Time: |
|-------|-------|
| Course: | |
| Par: | Distance: |
| Weather: | Wind: |

| Hole | 1 | 2 | 3 | 4 | 5 | 6 | 7 | 8 | 9 | Out |
|------|---|---|---|---|---|---|---|---|---|-----|
| Par | | | | | | | | | | |
| Distance | | | | | | | | | | |
| | | | | | | | | | | |
| | | | | | | | | | | |
| | | | | | | | | | | |
| | | | | | | | | | | |

| Hole | 10 | 11 | 12 | 13 | 14 | 15 | 16 | 17 | 18 | In | Total |
|------|----|----|----|----|----|----|----|----|----|----|-------|
| Par | | | | | | | | | | | |
| Distance | | | | | | | | | | | |
| | | | | | | | | | | | |
| | | | | | | | | | | | |
| | | | | | | | | | | | |
| | | | | | | | | | | | |

Notes: _____

_____

_____

_____

_____

# DISC GOLF SCORECARD

| Date: | | Time: | |
|---|---|---|---|
| Course: | | | |
| Par: | | Distance: | |
| Weather: | | Wind: | |

| Hole | 1 | 2 | 3 | 4 | 5 | 6 | 7 | 8 | 9 | Out |
|---|---|---|---|---|---|---|---|---|---|---|
| Par | | | | | | | | | | |
| Distance | | | | | | | | | | |
| | | | | | | | | | | |
| | | | | | | | | | | |
| | | | | | | | | | | |
| | | | | | | | | | | |

| Hole | 10 | 11 | 12 | 13 | 14 | 15 | 16 | 17 | 18 | In | Total |
|---|---|---|---|---|---|---|---|---|---|---|---|
| Par | | | | | | | | | | | |
| Distance | | | | | | | | | | | |
| | | | | | | | | | | | |
| | | | | | | | | | | | |
| | | | | | | | | | | | |
| | | | | | | | | | | | |

Notes: _____
_____
_____
_____
_____

# DISC GOLF SCORECARD

| Date: | | Time: |
|---|---|---|
| Course: | | |
| Par: | | Distance: |
| Weather: | | Wind: |

| Hole | 1 | 2 | 3 | 4 | 5 | 6 | 7 | 8 | 9 | Out |
|---|---|---|---|---|---|---|---|---|---|---|
| Par | | | | | | | | | | |
| Distance | | | | | | | | | | |
| | | | | | | | | | | |
| | | | | | | | | | | |
| | | | | | | | | | | |
| | | | | | | | | | | |

| Hole | 10 | 11 | 12 | 13 | 14 | 15 | 16 | 17 | 18 | In | Total |
|---|---|---|---|---|---|---|---|---|---|---|---|
| Par | | | | | | | | | | | |
| Distance | | | | | | | | | | | |
| | | | | | | | | | | | |
| | | | | | | | | | | | |
| | | | | | | | | | | | |
| | | | | | | | | | | | |

Notes: _____
_____
_____
_____
_____

# DISC GOLF SCORECARD

| Date: | | Time: | |
|---|---|---|---|
| Course: | | | |
| Par: | | Distance: | |
| Weather: | | Wind: | |

| Hole | 1 | 2 | 3 | 4 | 5 | 6 | 7 | 8 | 9 | Out |
|---|---|---|---|---|---|---|---|---|---|---|
| Par | | | | | | | | | | |
| Distance | | | | | | | | | | |
| | | | | | | | | | | |
| | | | | | | | | | | |
| | | | | | | | | | | |
| | | | | | | | | | | |

| Hole | 10 | 11 | 12 | 13 | 14 | 15 | 16 | 17 | 18 | In | Total |
|---|---|---|---|---|---|---|---|---|---|---|---|
| Par | | | | | | | | | | | |
| Distance | | | | | | | | | | | |
| | | | | | | | | | | | |
| | | | | | | | | | | | |
| | | | | | | | | | | | |
| | | | | | | | | | | | |

Notes: _____
_____
_____
_____
_____

# DISC GOLF SCORECARD

| Date: | | | | Time: | | | | | | |
|-------|-|-|-|-------|-|-|-|-|-|-|

Course:

| Par: | | | | Distance: | | | | | | |
|------|-|-|-|-----------|-|-|-|-|-|-|

| Weather: | | | | Wind: | | | | | | |
|----------|-|-|-|-------|-|-|-|-|-|-|

| Hole | 1 | 2 | 3 | 4 | 5 | 6 | 7 | 8 | 9 | Out |
|------|---|---|---|---|---|---|---|---|---|-----|
| Par | | | | | | | | | | |
| Distance | | | | | | | | | | |
| | | | | | | | | | | |
| | | | | | | | | | | |
| | | | | | | | | | | |
| | | | | | | | | | | |

| Hole | 10 | 11 | 12 | 13 | 14 | 15 | 16 | 17 | 18 | In | Total |
|------|----|----|----|----|----|----|----|----|----|----|-------|
| Par | | | | | | | | | | | |
| Distance | | | | | | | | | | | |
| | | | | | | | | | | | |
| | | | | | | | | | | | |
| | | | | | | | | | | | |
| | | | | | | | | | | | |

Notes: _____
_____
_____
_____
_____

# DISC GOLF SCORECARD

| Date: | | Time: | |
|-------|--|-------|--|
| Course: | | | |
| Par: | | Distance: | |
| Weather: | | Wind: | |

| Hole | 1 | 2 | 3 | 4 | 5 | 6 | 7 | 8 | 9 | Out |
|------|---|---|---|---|---|---|---|---|---|-----|
| Par | | | | | | | | | | |
| Distance | | | | | | | | | | |
| | | | | | | | | | | |
| | | | | | | | | | | |
| | | | | | | | | | | |
| | | | | | | | | | | |

| Hole | 10 | 11 | 12 | 13 | 14 | 15 | 16 | 17 | 18 | In | Total |
|------|----|----|----|----|----|----|----|----|----|----|-------|
| Par | | | | | | | | | | | |
| Distance | | | | | | | | | | | |
| | | | | | | | | | | | |
| | | | | | | | | | | | |
| | | | | | | | | | | | |
| | | | | | | | | | | | |

Notes: _____
_____
_____
_____
_____

# DISC GOLF SCORECARD

| Date: | | Time: | |
|-------|--|-------|--|
| Course: | | | |
| Par: | | Distance: | |
| Weather: | | Wind: | |

| Hole | 1 | 2 | 3 | 4 | 5 | 6 | 7 | 8 | 9 | Out |
|------|---|---|---|---|---|---|---|---|---|-----|
| Par | | | | | | | | | | |
| Distance | | | | | | | | | | |
| | | | | | | | | | | |
| | | | | | | | | | | |
| | | | | | | | | | | |
| | | | | | | | | | | |

| Hole | 10 | 11 | 12 | 13 | 14 | 15 | 16 | 17 | 18 | In | Total |
|------|----|----|----|----|----|----|----|----|----|----|-------|
| Par | | | | | | | | | | | |
| Distance | | | | | | | | | | | |
| | | | | | | | | | | | |
| | | | | | | | | | | | |
| | | | | | | | | | | | |
| | | | | | | | | | | | |

Notes: _____
_____
_____
_____
_____

# DISC GOLF SCORECARD

| Date: | | Time: | |
|---|---|---|---|
| Course: | | | |
| Par: | | Distance: | |
| Weather: | | Wind: | |

| Hole | 1 | 2 | 3 | 4 | 5 | 6 | 7 | 8 | 9 | Out |
|---|---|---|---|---|---|---|---|---|---|---|
| Par | | | | | | | | | | |
| Distance | | | | | | | | | | |
| | | | | | | | | | | |
| | | | | | | | | | | |
| | | | | | | | | | | |
| | | | | | | | | | | |

| Hole | 10 | 11 | 12 | 13 | 14 | 15 | 16 | 17 | 18 | In | Total |
|---|---|---|---|---|---|---|---|---|---|---|---|
| Par | | | | | | | | | | | |
| Distance | | | | | | | | | | | |
| | | | | | | | | | | | |
| | | | | | | | | | | | |
| | | | | | | | | | | | |
| | | | | | | | | | | | |

Notes: _____
_____
_____
_____
_____

# DISC GOLF SCORECARD

| Date: | Time: |
|---|---|
| Course: | |
| Par: | Distance: |
| Weather: | Wind: |

| Hole | 1 | 2 | 3 | 4 | 5 | 6 | 7 | 8 | 9 | Out |
|---|---|---|---|---|---|---|---|---|---|---|
| Par | | | | | | | | | | |
| Distance | | | | | | | | | | |
| | | | | | | | | | | |
| | | | | | | | | | | |
| | | | | | | | | | | |
| | | | | | | | | | | |

| Hole | 10 | 11 | 12 | 13 | 14 | 15 | 16 | 17 | 18 | In | Total |
|---|---|---|---|---|---|---|---|---|---|---|---|
| Par | | | | | | | | | | | |
| Distance | | | | | | | | | | | |
| | | | | | | | | | | | |
| | | | | | | | | | | | |
| | | | | | | | | | | | |
| | | | | | | | | | | | |

Notes: _____

_____

_____

_____

_____

# DISC GOLF SCORECARD

| Date: | | Time: | |
|---|---|---|---|
| Course: | | | |
| Par: | | Distance: | |
| Weather: | | Wind: | |

| Hole | 1 | 2 | 3 | 4 | 5 | 6 | 7 | 8 | 9 | Out |
|---|---|---|---|---|---|---|---|---|---|---|
| Par | | | | | | | | | | |
| Distance | | | | | | | | | | |
| | | | | | | | | | | |
| | | | | | | | | | | |
| | | | | | | | | | | |
| | | | | | | | | | | |

| Hole | 10 | 11 | 12 | 13 | 14 | 15 | 16 | 17 | 18 | In | Total |
|---|---|---|---|---|---|---|---|---|---|---|---|
| Par | | | | | | | | | | | |
| Distance | | | | | | | | | | | |
| | | | | | | | | | | | |
| | | | | | | | | | | | |
| | | | | | | | | | | | |
| | | | | | | | | | | | |

Notes: _____

_____

_____

_____

_____

# DISC GOLF SCORECARD

| Date: | | | | | | Time: | | | | |
|-------|--|--|--|--|--|-------|--|--|--|--|
| Course: | | | | | | | | | | |
| Par: | | | | | | Distance: | | | | |
| Weather: | | | | | | Wind: | | | | |

| Hole | 1 | 2 | 3 | 4 | 5 | 6 | 7 | 8 | 9 | Out |
|------|---|---|---|---|---|---|---|---|---|-----|
| Par | | | | | | | | | | |
| Distance | | | | | | | | | | |
| | | | | | | | | | | |
| | | | | | | | | | | |
| | | | | | | | | | | |
| | | | | | | | | | | |

| Hole | 10 | 11 | 12 | 13 | 14 | 15 | 16 | 17 | 18 | In | Total |
|------|----|----|----|----|----|----|----|----|----|----|-------|
| Par | | | | | | | | | | | |
| Distance | | | | | | | | | | | |
| | | | | | | | | | | | |
| | | | | | | | | | | | |
| | | | | | | | | | | | |
| | | | | | | | | | | | |

Notes: _____
_____
_____
_____

# DISC GOLF SCORECARD

| Date: | | | | | Time: | | | | |
|-------|-|-|-|-|-------|-|-|-|-|

| Course: | | | | | | | | | |
|---------|-|-|-|-|-|-|-|-|-|

| Par: | | | | | Distance: | | | | |
|------|-|-|-|-|-----------|-|-|-|-|

| Weather: | | | | | Wind: | | | | |
|----------|-|-|-|-|-------|-|-|-|-|

| Hole | 1 | 2 | 3 | 4 | 5 | 6 | 7 | 8 | 9 | Out |
|------|---|---|---|---|---|---|---|---|---|-----|
| Par | | | | | | | | | | |
| Distance | | | | | | | | | | |
| | | | | | | | | | | |
| | | | | | | | | | | |
| | | | | | | | | | | |
| | | | | | | | | | | |

| Hole | 10 | 11 | 12 | 13 | 14 | 15 | 16 | 17 | 18 | In | Total |
|------|----|----|----|----|----|----|----|----|----|----|-------|
| Par | | | | | | | | | | | |
| Distance | | | | | | | | | | | |
| | | | | | | | | | | | |
| | | | | | | | | | | | |
| | | | | | | | | | | | |
| | | | | | | | | | | | |

Notes: _____
_____
_____
_____
_____

# DISC GOLF SCORECARD

| Date: | Time: |
|---|---|
| Course: | |
| Par: | Distance: |
| Weather: | Wind: |

| Hole | 1 | 2 | 3 | 4 | 5 | 6 | 7 | 8 | 9 | Out |
|---|---|---|---|---|---|---|---|---|---|---|
| Par | | | | | | | | | | |
| Distance | | | | | | | | | | |
| | | | | | | | | | | |
| | | | | | | | | | | |
| | | | | | | | | | | |
| | | | | | | | | | | |

| Hole | 10 | 11 | 12 | 13 | 14 | 15 | 16 | 17 | 18 | In | Total |
|---|---|---|---|---|---|---|---|---|---|---|---|
| Par | | | | | | | | | | | |
| Distance | | | | | | | | | | | |
| | | | | | | | | | | | |
| | | | | | | | | | | | |
| | | | | | | | | | | | |
| | | | | | | | | | | | |

Notes: _____

_____

_____

_____

_____

# DISC GOLF SCORECARD

| Date: | | Time: | |
|-------|---|-------|---|
| Course: | | | |
| Par: | | Distance: | |
| Weather: | | Wind: | |

| Hole | 1 | 2 | 3 | 4 | 5 | 6 | 7 | 8 | 9 | Out |
|------|---|---|---|---|---|---|---|---|---|-----|
| Par | | | | | | | | | | |
| Distance | | | | | | | | | | |
| | | | | | | | | | | |
| | | | | | | | | | | |
| | | | | | | | | | | |
| | | | | | | | | | | |

| Hole | 10 | 11 | 12 | 13 | 14 | 15 | 16 | 17 | 18 | In | Total |
|------|----|----|----|----|----|----|----|----|----|----|-------|
| Par | | | | | | | | | | | |
| Distance | | | | | | | | | | | |
| | | | | | | | | | | | |
| | | | | | | | | | | | |
| | | | | | | | | | | | |
| | | | | | | | | | | | |

Notes: _____

_____

_____

_____

# DISC GOLF SCORECARD

| Date: | | Time: | |
|---|---|---|---|
| Course: | | | |
| Par: | | Distance: | |
| Weather: | | Wind: | |

| Hole | 1 | 2 | 3 | 4 | 5 | 6 | 7 | 8 | 9 | Out |
|---|---|---|---|---|---|---|---|---|---|---|
| Par | | | | | | | | | | |
| Distance | | | | | | | | | | |
| | | | | | | | | | | |
| | | | | | | | | | | |
| | | | | | | | | | | |
| | | | | | | | | | | |

| Hole | 10 | 11 | 12 | 13 | 14 | 15 | 16 | 17 | 18 | In | Total |
|---|---|---|---|---|---|---|---|---|---|---|---|
| Par | | | | | | | | | | | |
| Distance | | | | | | | | | | | |
| | | | | | | | | | | | |
| | | | | | | | | | | | |
| | | | | | | | | | | | |
| | | | | | | | | | | | |

Notes: _____

_____

_____

_____

# DISC GOLF SCORECARD

| Date: | | | | | Time: | | | | | |
|-------|---|---|---|---|-------|---|---|---|---|---|
| Course: | | | | | | | | | | |
| Par: | | | | | Distance: | | | | | |
| Weather: | | | | | Wind: | | | | | |

| Hole | 1 | 2 | 3 | 4 | 5 | 6 | 7 | 8 | 9 | Out |
|------|---|---|---|---|---|---|---|---|---|-----|
| Par | | | | | | | | | | |
| Distance | | | | | | | | | | |
| | | | | | | | | | | |
| | | | | | | | | | | |
| | | | | | | | | | | |
| | | | | | | | | | | |

| Hole | 10 | 11 | 12 | 13 | 14 | 15 | 16 | 17 | 18 | In | Total |
|------|----|----|----|----|----|----|----|----|----|----|-------|
| Par | | | | | | | | | | | |
| Distance | | | | | | | | | | | |
| | | | | | | | | | | | |
| | | | | | | | | | | | |
| | | | | | | | | | | | |
| | | | | | | | | | | | |

Notes: _____
_____
_____
_____
_____

# DISC GOLF SCORECARD

| Date: | Time: |
|-------|-------|
| Course: | |
| Par: | Distance: |
| Weather: | Wind: |

| Hole | 1 | 2 | 3 | 4 | 5 | 6 | 7 | 8 | 9 | Out |
|----------|---|---|---|---|---|---|---|---|---|-----|
| Par | | | | | | | | | | |
| Distance | | | | | | | | | | |
| | | | | | | | | | | |
| | | | | | | | | | | |
| | | | | | | | | | | |
| | | | | | | | | | | |

| Hole | 10 | 11 | 12 | 13 | 14 | 15 | 16 | 17 | 18 | In | Total |
|----------|----|----|----|----|----|----|----|----|----|----|-------|
| Par | | | | | | | | | | | |
| Distance | | | | | | | | | | | |
| | | | | | | | | | | | |
| | | | | | | | | | | | |
| | | | | | | | | | | | |
| | | | | | | | | | | | |

Notes: _____

_____

_____

_____

_____

# DISC GOLF SCORECARD

| Date: | Time: |
|---|---|
| Course: | |
| Par: | Distance: |
| Weather: | Wind: |

| Hole | 1 | 2 | 3 | 4 | 5 | 6 | 7 | 8 | 9 | Out |
|---|---|---|---|---|---|---|---|---|---|---|
| Par | | | | | | | | | | |
| Distance | | | | | | | | | | |
| | | | | | | | | | | |
| | | | | | | | | | | |
| | | | | | | | | | | |
| | | | | | | | | | | |

| Hole | 10 | 11 | 12 | 13 | 14 | 15 | 16 | 17 | 18 | In | Total |
|---|---|---|---|---|---|---|---|---|---|---|---|
| Par | | | | | | | | | | | |
| Distance | | | | | | | | | | | |
| | | | | | | | | | | | |
| | | | | | | | | | | | |
| | | | | | | | | | | | |
| | | | | | | | | | | | |

Notes: _____

_____

_____

_____

_____

# DISC GOLF SCORECARD

| Date: | | | | | Time: | | | | |
|-------|---|---|---|---|-------|---|---|---|---|
| Course: | | | | | | | | | |
| Par: | | | | | Distance: | | | | |
| Weather: | | | | | Wind: | | | | |

| Hole | 1 | 2 | 3 | 4 | 5 | 6 | 7 | 8 | 9 | Out |
|------|---|---|---|---|---|---|---|---|---|-----|
| Par | | | | | | | | | | |
| Distance | | | | | | | | | | |
| | | | | | | | | | | |
| | | | | | | | | | | |
| | | | | | | | | | | |
| | | | | | | | | | | |

| Hole | 10 | 11 | 12 | 13 | 14 | 15 | 16 | 17 | 18 | In | Total |
|------|----|----|----|----|----|----|----|----|----|----|-------|
| Par | | | | | | | | | | | |
| Distance | | | | | | | | | | | |
| | | | | | | | | | | | |
| | | | | | | | | | | | |
| | | | | | | | | | | | |
| | | | | | | | | | | | |

Notes: _____

_____

_____

_____

_____

# DISC GOLF SCORECARD

| Date: | Time: |
|---|---|
| Course: | |
| Par: | Distance: |
| Weather: | Wind: |

| Hole | 1 | 2 | 3 | 4 | 5 | 6 | 7 | 8 | 9 | Out |
|---|---|---|---|---|---|---|---|---|---|---|
| Par | | | | | | | | | | |
| Distance | | | | | | | | | | |
| | | | | | | | | | | |
| | | | | | | | | | | |
| | | | | | | | | | | |
| | | | | | | | | | | |

| Hole | 10 | 11 | 12 | 13 | 14 | 15 | 16 | 17 | 18 | In | Total |
|---|---|---|---|---|---|---|---|---|---|---|---|
| Par | | | | | | | | | | | |
| Distance | | | | | | | | | | | |
| | | | | | | | | | | | |
| | | | | | | | | | | | |
| | | | | | | | | | | | |
| | | | | | | | | | | | |

Notes: _____

_____

_____

_____

_____

# DISC GOLF SCORECARD

| Date: | | Time: | | |
|---|---|---|---|---|
| Course: | | | | |
| Par: | | Distance: | | |
| Weather: | | Wind: | | |

| Hole | 1 | 2 | 3 | 4 | 5 | 6 | 7 | 8 | 9 | Out |
|---|---|---|---|---|---|---|---|---|---|---|
| Par | | | | | | | | | | |
| Distance | | | | | | | | | | |
| | | | | | | | | | | |
| | | | | | | | | | | |
| | | | | | | | | | | |
| | | | | | | | | | | |

| Hole | 10 | 11 | 12 | 13 | 14 | 15 | 16 | 17 | 18 | In | Total |
|---|---|---|---|---|---|---|---|---|---|---|---|
| Par | | | | | | | | | | | |
| Distance | | | | | | | | | | | |
| | | | | | | | | | | | |
| | | | | | | | | | | | |
| | | | | | | | | | | | |
| | | | | | | | | | | | |

Notes: _____

_____

_____

_____

_____

# DISC GOLF SCORECARD

| Date: | Time: |
|---|---|

| Course: | |

| Par: | Distance: |

| Weather: | Wind: |

| Hole | 1 | 2 | 3 | 4 | 5 | 6 | 7 | 8 | 9 | Out |
|---|---|---|---|---|---|---|---|---|---|---|
| Par | | | | | | | | | | |
| Distance | | | | | | | | | | |
| | | | | | | | | | | |
| | | | | | | | | | | |
| | | | | | | | | | | |
| | | | | | | | | | | |

| Hole | 10 | 11 | 12 | 13 | 14 | 15 | 16 | 17 | 18 | In | Total |
|---|---|---|---|---|---|---|---|---|---|---|---|
| Par | | | | | | | | | | | |
| Distance | | | | | | | | | | | |
| | | | | | | | | | | | |
| | | | | | | | | | | | |
| | | | | | | | | | | | |
| | | | | | | | | | | | |

Notes: _____

_____

_____

_____

_____

# DISC GOLF SCORECARD

| Date: | | Time: | |
|-------|--|-------|--|
| Course: | | | |
| Par: | | Distance: | |
| Weather: | | Wind: | |

| Hole | 1 | 2 | 3 | 4 | 5 | 6 | 7 | 8 | 9 | Out |
|----------|---|---|---|---|---|---|---|---|---|-----|
| Par | | | | | | | | | | |
| Distance | | | | | | | | | | |
| | | | | | | | | | | |
| | | | | | | | | | | |
| | | | | | | | | | | |
| | | | | | | | | | | |

| Hole | 10 | 11 | 12 | 13 | 14 | 15 | 16 | 17 | 18 | In | Total |
|----------|----|----|----|----|----|----|----|----|----|----|-------|
| Par | | | | | | | | | | | |
| Distance | | | | | | | | | | | |
| | | | | | | | | | | | |
| | | | | | | | | | | | |
| | | | | | | | | | | | |
| | | | | | | | | | | | |

Notes: _____
_____
_____
_____
_____

# DISC GOLF SCORECARD

| Date: | | Time: | |
|---|---|---|---|
| Course: | | | |
| Par: | | Distance: | |
| Weather: | | Wind: | |

| Hole | 1 | 2 | 3 | 4 | 5 | 6 | 7 | 8 | 9 | Out |
|---|---|---|---|---|---|---|---|---|---|---|
| Par | | | | | | | | | | |
| Distance | | | | | | | | | | |
| | | | | | | | | | | |
| | | | | | | | | | | |
| | | | | | | | | | | |
| | | | | | | | | | | |

| Hole | 10 | 11 | 12 | 13 | 14 | 15 | 16 | 17 | 18 | In | Total |
|---|---|---|---|---|---|---|---|---|---|---|---|
| Par | | | | | | | | | | | |
| Distance | | | | | | | | | | | |
| | | | | | | | | | | | |
| | | | | | | | | | | | |
| | | | | | | | | | | | |
| | | | | | | | | | | | |

Notes: _____

_____

_____

_____

# DISC GOLF SCORECARD

| Date: | | Time: | |
|---|---|---|---|
| Course: | | | |
| Par: | | Distance: | |
| Weather: | | Wind: | |

| Hole | 1 | 2 | 3 | 4 | 5 | 6 | 7 | 8 | 9 | Out |
|---|---|---|---|---|---|---|---|---|---|---|
| Par | | | | | | | | | | |
| Distance | | | | | | | | | | |
| | | | | | | | | | | |
| | | | | | | | | | | |
| | | | | | | | | | | |
| | | | | | | | | | | |

| Hole | 10 | 11 | 12 | 13 | 14 | 15 | 16 | 17 | 18 | In | Total |
|---|---|---|---|---|---|---|---|---|---|---|---|
| Par | | | | | | | | | | | |
| Distance | | | | | | | | | | | |
| | | | | | | | | | | | |
| | | | | | | | | | | | |
| | | | | | | | | | | | |
| | | | | | | | | | | | |

Notes: _____
_____
_____
_____
_____

# DISC GOLF SCORECARD

| Date: | | Time: | |
|---|---|---|---|
| Course: | | | |
| Par: | | Distance: | |
| Weather: | | Wind: | |

| Hole | 1 | 2 | 3 | 4 | 5 | 6 | 7 | 8 | 9 | Out |
|---|---|---|---|---|---|---|---|---|---|---|
| Par | | | | | | | | | | |
| Distance | | | | | | | | | | |
| | | | | | | | | | | |
| | | | | | | | | | | |
| | | | | | | | | | | |
| | | | | | | | | | | |

| Hole | 10 | 11 | 12 | 13 | 14 | 15 | 16 | 17 | 18 | In | Total |
|---|---|---|---|---|---|---|---|---|---|---|---|
| Par | | | | | | | | | | | |
| Distance | | | | | | | | | | | |
| | | | | | | | | | | | |
| | | | | | | | | | | | |
| | | | | | | | | | | | |
| | | | | | | | | | | | |

Notes: _____
_____
_____
_____
_____

# DISC GOLF SCORECARD

| Date: | | Time: |
|---|---|---|
| Course: | | |
| Par: | | Distance: |
| Weather: | | Wind: |

| Hole | 1 | 2 | 3 | 4 | 5 | 6 | 7 | 8 | 9 | Out |
|---|---|---|---|---|---|---|---|---|---|---|
| Par | | | | | | | | | | |
| Distance | | | | | | | | | | |
| | | | | | | | | | | |
| | | | | | | | | | | |
| | | | | | | | | | | |
| | | | | | | | | | | |

| Hole | 10 | 11 | 12 | 13 | 14 | 15 | 16 | 17 | 18 | In | Total |
|---|---|---|---|---|---|---|---|---|---|---|---|
| Par | | | | | | | | | | | |
| Distance | | | | | | | | | | | |
| | | | | | | | | | | | |
| | | | | | | | | | | | |
| | | | | | | | | | | | |
| | | | | | | | | | | | |

Notes: _____

_____

_____

_____

_____

# DISC GOLF SCORECARD

| Date: | | | | | | | | Time: | | | |
|---|---|---|---|---|---|---|---|---|---|---|---|
| Course: | | | | | | | | | | | |
| Par: | | | | | | | | Distance: | | | |
| Weather: | | | | | | | | Wind: | | | |

| Hole | 1 | 2 | 3 | 4 | 5 | 6 | 7 | 8 | 9 | Out |
|---|---|---|---|---|---|---|---|---|---|---|
| Par | | | | | | | | | | |
| Distance | | | | | | | | | | |
| | | | | | | | | | | |
| | | | | | | | | | | |
| | | | | | | | | | | |
| | | | | | | | | | | |

| Hole | 10 | 11 | 12 | 13 | 14 | 15 | 16 | 17 | 18 | In | Total |
|---|---|---|---|---|---|---|---|---|---|---|---|
| Par | | | | | | | | | | | |
| Distance | | | | | | | | | | | |
| | | | | | | | | | | | |
| | | | | | | | | | | | |
| | | | | | | | | | | | |
| | | | | | | | | | | | |

Notes: _____

_____

_____

_____

_____

# DISC GOLF SCORECARD

| Date: | | Time: |
|---|---|---|
| Course: | | |
| Par: | | Distance: |
| Weather: | | Wind: |

| Hole | 1 | 2 | 3 | 4 | 5 | 6 | 7 | 8 | 9 | Out |
|---|---|---|---|---|---|---|---|---|---|---|
| Par | | | | | | | | | | |
| Distance | | | | | | | | | | |
| | | | | | | | | | | |
| | | | | | | | | | | |
| | | | | | | | | | | |
| | | | | | | | | | | |

| Hole | 10 | 11 | 12 | 13 | 14 | 15 | 16 | 17 | 18 | In | Total |
|---|---|---|---|---|---|---|---|---|---|---|---|
| Par | | | | | | | | | | | |
| Distance | | | | | | | | | | | |
| | | | | | | | | | | | |
| | | | | | | | | | | | |
| | | | | | | | | | | | |
| | | | | | | | | | | | |

Notes: _____

_____

_____

_____

_____

# DISC GOLF SCORECARD

| Date: | | | | | | Time: | | | | |
|-------|--|--|--|--|--|-------|--|--|--|--|

| Course: |
|---------|

| Par: | | | | | | Distance: | | | | |
|------|--|--|--|--|--|-----------|--|--|--|--|

| Weather: | | | | | | Wind: | | | | |
|----------|--|--|--|--|--|-------|--|--|--|--|

| Hole | 1 | 2 | 3 | 4 | 5 | 6 | 7 | 8 | 9 | Out |
|------|---|---|---|---|---|---|---|---|---|-----|
| Par | | | | | | | | | | |
| Distance | | | | | | | | | | |
| | | | | | | | | | | |
| | | | | | | | | | | |
| | | | | | | | | | | |
| | | | | | | | | | | |

| Hole | 10 | 11 | 12 | 13 | 14 | 15 | 16 | 17 | 18 | In | Total |
|------|----|----|----|----|----|----|----|----|----|----|-------|
| Par | | | | | | | | | | | |
| Distance | | | | | | | | | | | |
| | | | | | | | | | | | |
| | | | | | | | | | | | |
| | | | | | | | | | | | |
| | | | | | | | | | | | |

Notes: _____

_____

_____

_____

# DISC GOLF SCORECARD

| Date: | Time: |
|---|---|
| Course: | |
| Par: | Distance: |
| Weather: | Wind: |

| Hole | 1 | 2 | 3 | 4 | 5 | 6 | 7 | 8 | 9 | Out |
|---|---|---|---|---|---|---|---|---|---|---|
| Par | | | | | | | | | | |
| Distance | | | | | | | | | | |
| | | | | | | | | | | |
| | | | | | | | | | | |
| | | | | | | | | | | |
| | | | | | | | | | | |

| Hole | 10 | 11 | 12 | 13 | 14 | 15 | 16 | 17 | 18 | In | Total |
|---|---|---|---|---|---|---|---|---|---|---|---|
| Par | | | | | | | | | | | |
| Distance | | | | | | | | | | | |
| | | | | | | | | | | | |
| | | | | | | | | | | | |
| | | | | | | | | | | | |
| | | | | | | | | | | | |

Notes: _____

_____

_____

_____

_____

# DISC GOLF SCORECARD

| Date: | Time: |
|---|---|
| Course: | |
| Par: | Distance: |
| Weather: | Wind: |

| Hole | 1 | 2 | 3 | 4 | 5 | 6 | 7 | 8 | 9 | Out |
|---|---|---|---|---|---|---|---|---|---|---|
| Par | | | | | | | | | | |
| Distance | | | | | | | | | | |
| | | | | | | | | | | |
| | | | | | | | | | | |
| | | | | | | | | | | |
| | | | | | | | | | | |

| Hole | 10 | 11 | 12 | 13 | 14 | 15 | 16 | 17 | 18 | In | Total |
|---|---|---|---|---|---|---|---|---|---|---|---|
| Par | | | | | | | | | | | |
| Distance | | | | | | | | | | | |
| | | | | | | | | | | | |
| | | | | | | | | | | | |
| | | | | | | | | | | | |
| | | | | | | | | | | | |

Notes: _____
_____
_____
_____
_____

# DISC GOLF SCORECARD

| Date: | Time: |
|-------|-------|
| Course: | |
| Par: | Distance: |
| Weather: | Wind: |

| Hole | 1 | 2 | 3 | 4 | 5 | 6 | 7 | 8 | 9 | Out |
|------|---|---|---|---|---|---|---|---|---|-----|
| Par | | | | | | | | | | |
| Distance | | | | | | | | | | |
| | | | | | | | | | | |
| | | | | | | | | | | |
| | | | | | | | | | | |
| | | | | | | | | | | |

| Hole | 10 | 11 | 12 | 13 | 14 | 15 | 16 | 17 | 18 | In | Total |
|------|----|----|----|----|----|----|----|----|----|----|-------|
| Par | | | | | | | | | | | |
| Distance | | | | | | | | | | | |
| | | | | | | | | | | | |
| | | | | | | | | | | | |
| | | | | | | | | | | | |
| | | | | | | | | | | | |

Notes: _____
_____
_____
_____
_____

# DISC GOLF SCORECARD

| Date: | | Time: | |
|---|---|---|---|
| Course: | | | |
| Par: | | Distance: | |
| Weather: | | Wind: | |

| Hole | 1 | 2 | 3 | 4 | 5 | 6 | 7 | 8 | 9 | Out |
|---|---|---|---|---|---|---|---|---|---|---|
| Par | | | | | | | | | | |
| Distance | | | | | | | | | | |
| | | | | | | | | | | |
| | | | | | | | | | | |
| | | | | | | | | | | |
| | | | | | | | | | | |

| Hole | 10 | 11 | 12 | 13 | 14 | 15 | 16 | 17 | 18 | In | Total |
|---|---|---|---|---|---|---|---|---|---|---|---|
| Par | | | | | | | | | | | |
| Distance | | | | | | | | | | | |
| | | | | | | | | | | | |
| | | | | | | | | | | | |
| | | | | | | | | | | | |
| | | | | | | | | | | | |

Notes: _____
_____
_____
_____
_____

# DISC GOLF SCORECARD

| Date: | | | | | Time: | | | | |
|---|---|---|---|---|---|---|---|---|---|
| Course: | | | | | | | | | |
| Par: | | | | | Distance: | | | | |
| Weather: | | | | | Wind: | | | | |

| Hole | 1 | 2 | 3 | 4 | 5 | 6 | 7 | 8 | 9 | Out |
|---|---|---|---|---|---|---|---|---|---|---|
| Par | | | | | | | | | | |
| Distance | | | | | | | | | | |
| | | | | | | | | | | |
| | | | | | | | | | | |
| | | | | | | | | | | |
| | | | | | | | | | | |

| Hole | 10 | 11 | 12 | 13 | 14 | 15 | 16 | 17 | 18 | In | Total |
|---|---|---|---|---|---|---|---|---|---|---|---|
| Par | | | | | | | | | | | |
| Distance | | | | | | | | | | | |
| | | | | | | | | | | | |
| | | | | | | | | | | | |
| | | | | | | | | | | | |
| | | | | | | | | | | | |

Notes: _____

_____

_____

_____

_____

# DISC GOLF SCORECARD

| Date: | Time: |
|---|---|

| Course: | |
|---|---|

| Par: | Distance: |
|---|---|

| Weather: | Wind: |
|---|---|

| Hole | 1 | 2 | 3 | 4 | 5 | 6 | 7 | 8 | 9 | Out |
|---|---|---|---|---|---|---|---|---|---|---|
| Par | | | | | | | | | | |
| Distance | | | | | | | | | | |
| | | | | | | | | | | |
| | | | | | | | | | | |
| | | | | | | | | | | |

| Hole | 10 | 11 | 12 | 13 | 14 | 15 | 16 | 17 | 18 | In | Total |
|---|---|---|---|---|---|---|---|---|---|---|---|
| Par | | | | | | | | | | | |
| Distance | | | | | | | | | | | |
| | | | | | | | | | | | |
| | | | | | | | | | | | |
| | | | | | | | | | | | |

Notes: _____
_____
_____
_____
_____

# DISC GOLF SCORECARD

| Date: | | Time: | |
|-------|--|-------|--|
| Course: | | | |
| Par: | | Distance: | |
| Weather: | | Wind: | |

| Hole | 1 | 2 | 3 | 4 | 5 | 6 | 7 | 8 | 9 | Out |
|------|---|---|---|---|---|---|---|---|---|-----|
| Par | | | | | | | | | | |
| Distance | | | | | | | | | | |
| | | | | | | | | | | |
| | | | | | | | | | | |
| | | | | | | | | | | |
| | | | | | | | | | | |

| Hole | 10 | 11 | 12 | 13 | 14 | 15 | 16 | 17 | 18 | In | Total |
|------|----|----|----|----|----|----|----|----|----|----|-------|
| Par | | | | | | | | | | | |
| Distance | | | | | | | | | | | |
| | | | | | | | | | | | |
| | | | | | | | | | | | |
| | | | | | | | | | | | |
| | | | | | | | | | | | |

Notes: _____
_____
_____
_____
_____

# DISC GOLF SCORECARD

| Date: | | Time: | |
|---|---|---|---|
| Course: | | | |
| Par: | | Distance: | |
| Weather: | | Wind: | |

| Hole | 1 | 2 | 3 | 4 | 5 | 6 | 7 | 8 | 9 | Out |
|---|---|---|---|---|---|---|---|---|---|---|
| Par | | | | | | | | | | |
| Distance | | | | | | | | | | |
| | | | | | | | | | | |
| | | | | | | | | | | |
| | | | | | | | | | | |
| | | | | | | | | | | |

| Hole | 10 | 11 | 12 | 13 | 14 | 15 | 16 | 17 | 18 | In | Total |
|---|---|---|---|---|---|---|---|---|---|---|---|
| Par | | | | | | | | | | | |
| Distance | | | | | | | | | | | |
| | | | | | | | | | | | |
| | | | | | | | | | | | |
| | | | | | | | | | | | |
| | | | | | | | | | | | |

Notes: _____

_____

_____

_____

_____

# DISC GOLF SCORECARD

| Date: | | Time: | |
|-------|--|-------|--|
| Course: | | | |
| Par: | | Distance: | |
| Weather: | | Wind: | |

| Hole | 1 | 2 | 3 | 4 | 5 | 6 | 7 | 8 | 9 | Out |
|------|---|---|---|---|---|---|---|---|---|-----|
| Par | | | | | | | | | | |
| Distance | | | | | | | | | | |
| | | | | | | | | | | |
| | | | | | | | | | | |
| | | | | | | | | | | |
| | | | | | | | | | | |

| Hole | 10 | 11 | 12 | 13 | 14 | 15 | 16 | 17 | 18 | In | Total |
|------|----|----|----|----|----|----|----|----|----|----|-------|
| Par | | | | | | | | | | | |
| Distance | | | | | | | | | | | |
| | | | | | | | | | | | |
| | | | | | | | | | | | |
| | | | | | | | | | | | |
| | | | | | | | | | | | |

Notes: _____
_____
_____
_____
_____

# DISC GOLF SCORECARD

| Date: | | | | | | Time: | | | | |
|-------|---|---|---|---|---|-------|---|---|---|---|
| Course: | | | | | | | | | | |
| Par: | | | | | | Distance: | | | | |
| Weather: | | | | | | Wind: | | | | |

| Hole | 1 | 2 | 3 | 4 | 5 | 6 | 7 | 8 | 9 | Out |
|------|---|---|---|---|---|---|---|---|---|-----|
| Par | | | | | | | | | | |
| Distance | | | | | | | | | | |
| | | | | | | | | | | |
| | | | | | | | | | | |
| | | | | | | | | | | |
| | | | | | | | | | | |

| Hole | 10 | 11 | 12 | 13 | 14 | 15 | 16 | 17 | 18 | In | Total |
|------|----|----|----|----|----|----|----|----|----|----|-------|
| Par | | | | | | | | | | | |
| Distance | | | | | | | | | | | |
| | | | | | | | | | | | |
| | | | | | | | | | | | |
| | | | | | | | | | | | |
| | | | | | | | | | | | |

Notes: _____
_____
_____
_____
_____

# DISC GOLF SCORECARD

| Date: | Time: |
|---|---|
| Course: | |
| Par: | Distance: |
| Weather: | Wind: |

| Hole | 1 | 2 | 3 | 4 | 5 | 6 | 7 | 8 | 9 | Out |
|---|---|---|---|---|---|---|---|---|---|---|
| Par | | | | | | | | | | |
| Distance | | | | | | | | | | |
| | | | | | | | | | | |
| | | | | | | | | | | |
| | | | | | | | | | | |
| | | | | | | | | | | |

| Hole | 10 | 11 | 12 | 13 | 14 | 15 | 16 | 17 | 18 | In | Total |
|---|---|---|---|---|---|---|---|---|---|---|---|
| Par | | | | | | | | | | | |
| Distance | | | | | | | | | | | |
| | | | | | | | | | | | |
| | | | | | | | | | | | |
| | | | | | | | | | | | |
| | | | | | | | | | | | |

Notes: _____
_____
_____
_____
_____

# DISC GOLF SCORECARD

| Date: | | Time: | |
|---|---|---|---|

| Course: | |
|---|---|

| Par: | | Distance: | |
|---|---|---|---|

| Weather: | | Wind: | |
|---|---|---|---|

| Hole | 1 | 2 | 3 | 4 | 5 | 6 | 7 | 8 | 9 | Out |
|---|---|---|---|---|---|---|---|---|---|---|
| Par | | | | | | | | | | |
| Distance | | | | | | | | | | |
| | | | | | | | | | | |
| | | | | | | | | | | |
| | | | | | | | | | | |
| | | | | | | | | | | |

| Hole | 10 | 11 | 12 | 13 | 14 | 15 | 16 | 17 | 18 | In | Total |
|---|---|---|---|---|---|---|---|---|---|---|---|
| Par | | | | | | | | | | | |
| Distance | | | | | | | | | | | |
| | | | | | | | | | | | |
| | | | | | | | | | | | |
| | | | | | | | | | | | |
| | | | | | | | | | | | |

Notes: _____

_____

_____

_____

_____

# DISC GOLF SCORECARD

| Date: | Time: |
|---|---|
| Course: | |
| Par: | Distance: |
| Weather: | Wind: |

| Hole | 1 | 2 | 3 | 4 | 5 | 6 | 7 | 8 | 9 | Out |
|---|---|---|---|---|---|---|---|---|---|---|
| Par | | | | | | | | | | |
| Distance | | | | | | | | | | |
| | | | | | | | | | | |
| | | | | | | | | | | |
| | | | | | | | | | | |
| | | | | | | | | | | |

| Hole | 10 | 11 | 12 | 13 | 14 | 15 | 16 | 17 | 18 | In | Total |
|---|---|---|---|---|---|---|---|---|---|---|---|
| Par | | | | | | | | | | | |
| Distance | | | | | | | | | | | |
| | | | | | | | | | | | |
| | | | | | | | | | | | |
| | | | | | | | | | | | |
| | | | | | | | | | | | |

Notes: _____

_____

_____

_____

_____

# DISC GOLF SCORECARD

| Date: | | Time: | |
|---|---|---|---|
| Course: | | | |
| Par: | | Distance: | |
| Weather: | | Wind: | |

| Hole | 1 | 2 | 3 | 4 | 5 | 6 | 7 | 8 | 9 | Out |
|---|---|---|---|---|---|---|---|---|---|---|
| Par | | | | | | | | | | |
| Distance | | | | | | | | | | |
| | | | | | | | | | | |
| | | | | | | | | | | |
| | | | | | | | | | | |
| | | | | | | | | | | |

| Hole | 10 | 11 | 12 | 13 | 14 | 15 | 16 | 17 | 18 | In | Total |
|---|---|---|---|---|---|---|---|---|---|---|---|
| Par | | | | | | | | | | | |
| Distance | | | | | | | | | | | |
| | | | | | | | | | | | |
| | | | | | | | | | | | |
| | | | | | | | | | | | |
| | | | | | | | | | | | |

Notes: _____

_____

_____

_____

_____

# DISC GOLF SCORECARD

| Date: | | Time: | |
|---|---|---|---|
| Course: | | | |
| Par: | | Distance: | |
| Weather: | | Wind: | |

| Hole | 1 | 2 | 3 | 4 | 5 | 6 | 7 | 8 | 9 | Out |
|---|---|---|---|---|---|---|---|---|---|---|
| Par | | | | | | | | | | |
| Distance | | | | | | | | | | |
| | | | | | | | | | | |
| | | | | | | | | | | |
| | | | | | | | | | | |
| | | | | | | | | | | |

| Hole | 10 | 11 | 12 | 13 | 14 | 15 | 16 | 17 | 18 | In | Total |
|---|---|---|---|---|---|---|---|---|---|---|---|
| Par | | | | | | | | | | | |
| Distance | | | | | | | | | | | |
| | | | | | | | | | | | |
| | | | | | | | | | | | |
| | | | | | | | | | | | |
| | | | | | | | | | | | |

Notes: _____
_____
_____
_____
_____

# DISC GOLF SCORECARD

| Date: | Time: |
|---|---|
| Course: | |
| Par: | Distance: |
| Weather: | Wind: |

| Hole | 1 | 2 | 3 | 4 | 5 | 6 | 7 | 8 | 9 | Out |
|---|---|---|---|---|---|---|---|---|---|---|
| Par | | | | | | | | | | |
| Distance | | | | | | | | | | |
| | | | | | | | | | | |
| | | | | | | | | | | |
| | | | | | | | | | | |
| | | | | | | | | | | |

| Hole | 10 | 11 | 12 | 13 | 14 | 15 | 16 | 17 | 18 | In | Total |
|---|---|---|---|---|---|---|---|---|---|---|---|
| Par | | | | | | | | | | | |
| Distance | | | | | | | | | | | |
| | | | | | | | | | | | |
| | | | | | | | | | | | |
| | | | | | | | | | | | |
| | | | | | | | | | | | |

Notes: _____
_____
_____
_____
_____

# DISC GOLF SCORECARD

| Date: | | Time: | |
|---|---|---|---|
| Course: | | | |
| Par: | | Distance: | |
| Weather: | | Wind: | |

| Hole | 1 | 2 | 3 | 4 | 5 | 6 | 7 | 8 | 9 | Out |
|---|---|---|---|---|---|---|---|---|---|---|
| Par | | | | | | | | | | |
| Distance | | | | | | | | | | |
| | | | | | | | | | | |
| | | | | | | | | | | |
| | | | | | | | | | | |
| | | | | | | | | | | |

| Hole | 10 | 11 | 12 | 13 | 14 | 15 | 16 | 17 | 18 | In | Total |
|---|---|---|---|---|---|---|---|---|---|---|---|
| Par | | | | | | | | | | | |
| Distance | | | | | | | | | | | |
| | | | | | | | | | | | |
| | | | | | | | | | | | |
| | | | | | | | | | | | |
| | | | | | | | | | | | |

Notes: _____

_____

_____

_____

_____

# DISC GOLF SCORECARD

| Date: | | Time: | |
|---|---|---|---|
| Course: | | | |
| Par: | | Distance: | |
| Weather: | | Wind: | |

| Hole | 1 | 2 | 3 | 4 | 5 | 6 | 7 | 8 | 9 | Out |
|---|---|---|---|---|---|---|---|---|---|---|
| Par | | | | | | | | | | |
| Distance | | | | | | | | | | |
| | | | | | | | | | | |
| | | | | | | | | | | |
| | | | | | | | | | | |
| | | | | | | | | | | |

| Hole | 10 | 11 | 12 | 13 | 14 | 15 | 16 | 17 | 18 | In | Total |
|---|---|---|---|---|---|---|---|---|---|---|---|
| Par | | | | | | | | | | | |
| Distance | | | | | | | | | | | |
| | | | | | | | | | | | |
| | | | | | | | | | | | |
| | | | | | | | | | | | |
| | | | | | | | | | | | |

Notes: _____
_____
_____
_____
_____

# DISC GOLF SCORECARD

| Date: | | Time: | |
|-------|---|-------|---|
| Course: | | | |
| Par: | | Distance: | |
| Weather: | | Wind: | |

| Hole | 1 | 2 | 3 | 4 | 5 | 6 | 7 | 8 | 9 | Out |
|------|---|---|---|---|---|---|---|---|---|-----|
| Par | | | | | | | | | | |
| Distance | | | | | | | | | | |
| | | | | | | | | | | |
| | | | | | | | | | | |
| | | | | | | | | | | |
| | | | | | | | | | | |

| Hole | 10 | 11 | 12 | 13 | 14 | 15 | 16 | 17 | 18 | In | Total |
|------|----|----|----|----|----|----|----|----|----|----|-------|
| Par | | | | | | | | | | | |
| Distance | | | | | | | | | | | |
| | | | | | | | | | | | |
| | | | | | | | | | | | |
| | | | | | | | | | | | |
| | | | | | | | | | | | |

Notes: _____

_____

_____

_____

_____

# DISC GOLF SCORECARD

| Date: | | Time: | |
|---|---|---|---|
| Course: | | | |
| Par: | | Distance: | |
| Weather: | | Wind: | |

| Hole | 1 | 2 | 3 | 4 | 5 | 6 | 7 | 8 | 9 | Out |
|---|---|---|---|---|---|---|---|---|---|---|
| Par | | | | | | | | | | |
| Distance | | | | | | | | | | |
| | | | | | | | | | | |
| | | | | | | | | | | |
| | | | | | | | | | | |
| | | | | | | | | | | |

| Hole | 10 | 11 | 12 | 13 | 14 | 15 | 16 | 17 | 18 | In | Total |
|---|---|---|---|---|---|---|---|---|---|---|---|
| Par | | | | | | | | | | | |
| Distance | | | | | | | | | | | |
| | | | | | | | | | | | |
| | | | | | | | | | | | |
| | | | | | | | | | | | |
| | | | | | | | | | | | |

Notes: _____
_____
_____
_____
_____

# DISC GOLF SCORECARD

| Date: | | | | Time: | | | | | | |
|---|---|---|---|---|---|---|---|---|---|---|
| Course: | | | | | | | | | | |
| Par: | | | | Distance: | | | | | | |
| Weather: | | | | Wind: | | | | | | |

| Hole | 1 | 2 | 3 | 4 | 5 | 6 | 7 | 8 | 9 | Out |
|---|---|---|---|---|---|---|---|---|---|---|
| Par | | | | | | | | | | |
| Distance | | | | | | | | | | |
| | | | | | | | | | | |
| | | | | | | | | | | |
| | | | | | | | | | | |
| | | | | | | | | | | |

| Hole | 10 | 11 | 12 | 13 | 14 | 15 | 16 | 17 | 18 | In | Total |
|---|---|---|---|---|---|---|---|---|---|---|---|
| Par | | | | | | | | | | | |
| Distance | | | | | | | | | | | |
| | | | | | | | | | | | |
| | | | | | | | | | | | |
| | | | | | | | | | | | |
| | | | | | | | | | | | |

Notes: _____

_____

_____

_____

_____

# DISC GOLF SCORECARD

| Date: | Time: |
|---|---|
| Course: | |
| Par: | Distance: |
| Weather: | Wind: |

| Hole | 1 | 2 | 3 | 4 | 5 | 6 | 7 | 8 | 9 | Out |
|---|---|---|---|---|---|---|---|---|---|---|
| Par | | | | | | | | | | |
| Distance | | | | | | | | | | |
| | | | | | | | | | | |
| | | | | | | | | | | |
| | | | | | | | | | | |
| | | | | | | | | | | |

| Hole | 10 | 11 | 12 | 13 | 14 | 15 | 16 | 17 | 18 | In | Total |
|---|---|---|---|---|---|---|---|---|---|---|---|
| Par | | | | | | | | | | | |
| Distance | | | | | | | | | | | |
| | | | | | | | | | | | |
| | | | | | | | | | | | |
| | | | | | | | | | | | |
| | | | | | | | | | | | |

Notes: _____
_____
_____
_____
_____

# DISC GOLF SCORECARD

| Date: | | Time: | |
|---|---|---|---|
| Course: | | | |
| Par: | | Distance: | |
| Weather: | | Wind: | |

| Hole | 1 | 2 | 3 | 4 | 5 | 6 | 7 | 8 | 9 | Out |
|---|---|---|---|---|---|---|---|---|---|---|
| Par | | | | | | | | | | |
| Distance | | | | | | | | | | |
| | | | | | | | | | | |
| | | | | | | | | | | |
| | | | | | | | | | | |
| | | | | | | | | | | |

| Hole | 10 | 11 | 12 | 13 | 14 | 15 | 16 | 17 | 18 | In | Total |
|---|---|---|---|---|---|---|---|---|---|---|---|
| Par | | | | | | | | | | | |
| Distance | | | | | | | | | | | |
| | | | | | | | | | | | |
| | | | | | | | | | | | |
| | | | | | | | | | | | |
| | | | | | | | | | | | |

Notes: _____

_____

_____

_____

_____

# DISC GOLF SCORECARD

| Date: | | Time: | |
|-------|--|-------|--|
| Course: | | | |
| Par: | | Distance: | |
| Weather: | | Wind: | |

| Hole | 1 | 2 | 3 | 4 | 5 | 6 | 7 | 8 | 9 | Out |
|------|---|---|---|---|---|---|---|---|---|-----|
| Par | | | | | | | | | | |
| Distance | | | | | | | | | | |
| | | | | | | | | | | |
| | | | | | | | | | | |
| | | | | | | | | | | |
| | | | | | | | | | | |

| Hole | 10 | 11 | 12 | 13 | 14 | 15 | 16 | 17 | 18 | In | Total |
|------|----|----|----|----|----|----|----|----|----|----|-------|
| Par | | | | | | | | | | | |
| Distance | | | | | | | | | | | |
| | | | | | | | | | | | |
| | | | | | | | | | | | |
| | | | | | | | | | | | |
| | | | | | | | | | | | |

Notes: _____

_____

_____

_____

_____

# DISC GOLF SCORECARD

| Date: | | Time: |
|---|---|---|
| Course: | | |
| Par: | | Distance: |
| Weather: | | Wind: |

| Hole | 1 | 2 | 3 | 4 | 5 | 6 | 7 | 8 | 9 | Out |
|---|---|---|---|---|---|---|---|---|---|---|
| Par | | | | | | | | | | |
| Distance | | | | | | | | | | |
| | | | | | | | | | | |
| | | | | | | | | | | |
| | | | | | | | | | | |
| | | | | | | | | | | |

| Hole | 10 | 11 | 12 | 13 | 14 | 15 | 16 | 17 | 18 | In | Total |
|---|---|---|---|---|---|---|---|---|---|---|---|
| Par | | | | | | | | | | | |
| Distance | | | | | | | | | | | |
| | | | | | | | | | | | |
| | | | | | | | | | | | |
| | | | | | | | | | | | |
| | | | | | | | | | | | |

Notes: _____

_____

_____

_____

_____

# DISC GOLF SCORECARD

| Date: | | Time: | |
|---|---|---|---|
| Course: | | | |
| Par: | | Distance: | |
| Weather: | | Wind: | |

| Hole | 1 | 2 | 3 | 4 | 5 | 6 | 7 | 8 | 9 | Out |
|---|---|---|---|---|---|---|---|---|---|---|
| Par | | | | | | | | | | |
| Distance | | | | | | | | | | |
| | | | | | | | | | | |
| | | | | | | | | | | |
| | | | | | | | | | | |
| | | | | | | | | | | |

| Hole | 10 | 11 | 12 | 13 | 14 | 15 | 16 | 17 | 18 | In | Total |
|---|---|---|---|---|---|---|---|---|---|---|---|
| Par | | | | | | | | | | | |
| Distance | | | | | | | | | | | |
| | | | | | | | | | | | |
| | | | | | | | | | | | |
| | | | | | | | | | | | |
| | | | | | | | | | | | |

Notes: _____
_____
_____
_____
_____

# DISC GOLF SCORECARD

| Date: | | Time: |
|---|---|---|
| Course: | | |
| Par: | | Distance: |
| Weather: | | Wind: |

| Hole | 1 | 2 | 3 | 4 | 5 | 6 | 7 | 8 | 9 | Out |
|---|---|---|---|---|---|---|---|---|---|---|
| Par | | | | | | | | | | |
| Distance | | | | | | | | | | |
| | | | | | | | | | | |
| | | | | | | | | | | |
| | | | | | | | | | | |
| | | | | | | | | | | |

| Hole | 10 | 11 | 12 | 13 | 14 | 15 | 16 | 17 | 18 | In | Total |
|---|---|---|---|---|---|---|---|---|---|---|---|
| Par | | | | | | | | | | | |
| Distance | | | | | | | | | | | |
| | | | | | | | | | | | |
| | | | | | | | | | | | |
| | | | | | | | | | | | |
| | | | | | | | | | | | |

Notes: _____

_____

_____

_____

_____

# DISC GOLF SCORECARD

| Date: | | | | | | | | Time: | | | |
|-------|--|--|--|--|--|--|--|-------|--|--|--|
| Course: | | | | | | | | | | | |
| Par: | | | | | | | | Distance: | | | |
| Weather: | | | | | | | | Wind: | | | |

| Hole | 1 | 2 | 3 | 4 | 5 | 6 | 7 | 8 | 9 | Out |
|------|---|---|---|---|---|---|---|---|---|-----|
| Par | | | | | | | | | | |
| Distance | | | | | | | | | | |
| | | | | | | | | | | |
| | | | | | | | | | | |
| | | | | | | | | | | |
| | | | | | | | | | | |

| Hole | 10 | 11 | 12 | 13 | 14 | 15 | 16 | 17 | 18 | In | Total |
|------|----|----|----|----|----|----|----|----|----|----|-------|
| Par | | | | | | | | | | | |
| Distance | | | | | | | | | | | |
| | | | | | | | | | | | |
| | | | | | | | | | | | |
| | | | | | | | | | | | |
| | | | | | | | | | | | |

Notes: _____
_____
_____
_____
_____

# DISC GOLF SCORECARD

| Date: | | Time: | |
|---|---|---|---|
| Course: | | | |
| Par: | | Distance: | |
| Weather: | | Wind: | |

| Hole | 1 | 2 | 3 | 4 | 5 | 6 | 7 | 8 | 9 | Out |
|---|---|---|---|---|---|---|---|---|---|---|
| Par | | | | | | | | | | |
| Distance | | | | | | | | | | |
| | | | | | | | | | | |
| | | | | | | | | | | |
| | | | | | | | | | | |
| | | | | | | | | | | |

| Hole | 10 | 11 | 12 | 13 | 14 | 15 | 16 | 17 | 18 | In | Total |
|---|---|---|---|---|---|---|---|---|---|---|---|
| Par | | | | | | | | | | | |
| Distance | | | | | | | | | | | |
| | | | | | | | | | | | |
| | | | | | | | | | | | |
| | | | | | | | | | | | |
| | | | | | | | | | | | |

Notes: _____
_____
_____
_____
_____

# DISC GOLF SCORECARD

| Date: | | | | | Time: | | | | |
|---|---|---|---|---|---|---|---|---|---|
| Course: | | | | | | | | | |
| Par: | | | | | Distance: | | | | |
| Weather: | | | | | Wind: | | | | |

| Hole | 1 | 2 | 3 | 4 | 5 | 6 | 7 | 8 | 9 | Out |
|---|---|---|---|---|---|---|---|---|---|---|
| Par | | | | | | | | | | |
| Distance | | | | | | | | | | |
| | | | | | | | | | | |
| | | | | | | | | | | |
| | | | | | | | | | | |
| | | | | | | | | | | |

| Hole | 10 | 11 | 12 | 13 | 14 | 15 | 16 | 17 | 18 | In | Total |
|---|---|---|---|---|---|---|---|---|---|---|---|
| Par | | | | | | | | | | | |
| Distance | | | | | | | | | | | |
| | | | | | | | | | | | |
| | | | | | | | | | | | |
| | | | | | | | | | | | |
| | | | | | | | | | | | |

Notes: _____

_____

_____

_____

_____

# DISC GOLF SCORECARD

| Date: | Time: |
|-------|-------|
| Course: | |
| Par: | Distance: |
| Weather: | Wind: |

| Hole | 1 | 2 | 3 | 4 | 5 | 6 | 7 | 8 | 9 | Out |
|------|---|---|---|---|---|---|---|---|---|-----|
| Par | | | | | | | | | | |
| Distance | | | | | | | | | | |
| | | | | | | | | | | |
| | | | | | | | | | | |
| | | | | | | | | | | |
| | | | | | | | | | | |

| Hole | 10 | 11 | 12 | 13 | 14 | 15 | 16 | 17 | 18 | In | Total |
|------|----|----|----|----|----|----|----|----|----|----|-------|
| Par | | | | | | | | | | | |
| Distance | | | | | | | | | | | |
| | | | | | | | | | | | |
| | | | | | | | | | | | |
| | | | | | | | | | | | |
| | | | | | | | | | | | |

Notes: _____

_____

_____

_____

_____

# DISC GOLF SCORECARD

| Date: | Time: |
|---|---|

| Course: |
|---|

| Par: | Distance: |
|---|---|

| Weather: | Wind: |
|---|---|

| Hole | 1 | 2 | 3 | 4 | 5 | 6 | 7 | 8 | 9 | Out |
|---|---|---|---|---|---|---|---|---|---|---|
| Par | | | | | | | | | | |
| Distance | | | | | | | | | | |
| | | | | | | | | | | |
| | | | | | | | | | | |
| | | | | | | | | | | |
| | | | | | | | | | | |

| Hole | 10 | 11 | 12 | 13 | 14 | 15 | 16 | 17 | 18 | In | Total |
|---|---|---|---|---|---|---|---|---|---|---|---|
| Par | | | | | | | | | | | |
| Distance | | | | | | | | | | | |
| | | | | | | | | | | | |
| | | | | | | | | | | | |
| | | | | | | | | | | | |
| | | | | | | | | | | | |

Notes: _____
_____
_____
_____
_____

# DISC GOLF SCORECARD

| Date: | Time: |
|-------|-------|
| Course: | |
| Par: | Distance: |
| Weather: | Wind: |

| Hole | 1 | 2 | 3 | 4 | 5 | 6 | 7 | 8 | 9 | Out |
|------|---|---|---|---|---|---|---|---|---|-----|
| Par | | | | | | | | | | |
| Distance | | | | | | | | | | |
| | | | | | | | | | | |
| | | | | | | | | | | |
| | | | | | | | | | | |
| | | | | | | | | | | |

| Hole | 10 | 11 | 12 | 13 | 14 | 15 | 16 | 17 | 18 | In | Total |
|------|----|----|----|----|----|----|----|----|----|----|-------|
| Par | | | | | | | | | | | |
| Distance | | | | | | | | | | | |
| | | | | | | | | | | | |
| | | | | | | | | | | | |
| | | | | | | | | | | | |
| | | | | | | | | | | | |

Notes: _____

_____

_____

_____

_____

# DISC GOLF SCORECARD

| Date: | | Time: | |
|---|---|---|---|
| Course: | | | |
| Par: | | Distance: | |
| Weather: | | Wind: | |

| Hole | 1 | 2 | 3 | 4 | 5 | 6 | 7 | 8 | 9 | Out |
|---|---|---|---|---|---|---|---|---|---|---|
| Par | | | | | | | | | | |
| Distance | | | | | | | | | | |
| | | | | | | | | | | |
| | | | | | | | | | | |
| | | | | | | | | | | |
| | | | | | | | | | | |

| Hole | 10 | 11 | 12 | 13 | 14 | 15 | 16 | 17 | 18 | In | Total |
|---|---|---|---|---|---|---|---|---|---|---|---|
| Par | | | | | | | | | | | |
| Distance | | | | | | | | | | | |
| | | | | | | | | | | | |
| | | | | | | | | | | | |
| | | | | | | | | | | | |
| | | | | | | | | | | | |

Notes: _____
_____
_____
_____
_____

# DISC GOLF SCORECARD

| Date: | Time: |
|---|---|
| Course: | |
| Par: | Distance: |
| Weather: | Wind: |

| Hole | 1 | 2 | 3 | 4 | 5 | 6 | 7 | 8 | 9 | Out |
|---|---|---|---|---|---|---|---|---|---|---|
| Par | | | | | | | | | | |
| Distance | | | | | | | | | | |
| | | | | | | | | | | |
| | | | | | | | | | | |
| | | | | | | | | | | |
| | | | | | | | | | | |

| Hole | 10 | 11 | 12 | 13 | 14 | 15 | 16 | 17 | 18 | In | Total |
|---|---|---|---|---|---|---|---|---|---|---|---|
| Par | | | | | | | | | | | |
| Distance | | | | | | | | | | | |
| | | | | | | | | | | | |
| | | | | | | | | | | | |
| | | | | | | | | | | | |
| | | | | | | | | | | | |

Notes: _____

_____

_____

_____

_____

# DISC GOLF SCORECARD

| Date: | | Time: | |
|---|---|---|---|
| Course: | | | |
| Par: | | Distance: | |
| Weather: | | Wind: | |

| Hole | 1 | 2 | 3 | 4 | 5 | 6 | 7 | 8 | 9 | Out |
|---|---|---|---|---|---|---|---|---|---|---|
| Par | | | | | | | | | | |
| Distance | | | | | | | | | | |
| | | | | | | | | | | |
| | | | | | | | | | | |
| | | | | | | | | | | |
| | | | | | | | | | | |

| Hole | 10 | 11 | 12 | 13 | 14 | 15 | 16 | 17 | 18 | In | Total |
|---|---|---|---|---|---|---|---|---|---|---|---|
| Par | | | | | | | | | | | |
| Distance | | | | | | | | | | | |
| | | | | | | | | | | | |
| | | | | | | | | | | | |
| | | | | | | | | | | | |
| | | | | | | | | | | | |

Notes: _____
_____
_____
_____
_____

# DISC GOLF SCORECARD

| Date: | | Time: | |
|-------|--|-------|--|
| Course: | | | |
| Par: | | Distance: | |
| Weather: | | Wind: | |

| Hole | 1 | 2 | 3 | 4 | 5 | 6 | 7 | 8 | 9 | Out |
|----------|---|---|---|---|---|---|---|---|---|-----|
| Par | | | | | | | | | | |
| Distance | | | | | | | | | | |
| | | | | | | | | | | |
| | | | | | | | | | | |
| | | | | | | | | | | |
| | | | | | | | | | | |

| Hole | 10 | 11 | 12 | 13 | 14 | 15 | 16 | 17 | 18 | In | Total |
|----------|----|----|----|----|----|----|----|----|----|----|-------|
| Par | | | | | | | | | | | |
| Distance | | | | | | | | | | | |
| | | | | | | | | | | | |
| | | | | | | | | | | | |
| | | | | | | | | | | | |
| | | | | | | | | | | | |

Notes: _____

_____

_____

_____

_____

# DISC GOLF SCORECARD

| Date: | | Time: | |
|---|---|---|---|
| Course: | | | |
| Par: | | Distance: | |
| Weather: | | Wind: | |

| Hole | 1 | 2 | 3 | 4 | 5 | 6 | 7 | 8 | 9 | Out |
|---|---|---|---|---|---|---|---|---|---|---|
| Par | | | | | | | | | | |
| Distance | | | | | | | | | | |
| | | | | | | | | | | |
| | | | | | | | | | | |
| | | | | | | | | | | |
| | | | | | | | | | | |

| Hole | 10 | 11 | 12 | 13 | 14 | 15 | 16 | 17 | 18 | In | Total |
|---|---|---|---|---|---|---|---|---|---|---|---|
| Par | | | | | | | | | | | |
| Distance | | | | | | | | | | | |
| | | | | | | | | | | | |
| | | | | | | | | | | | |
| | | | | | | | | | | | |
| | | | | | | | | | | | |

Notes: _____

_____

_____

_____

_____

# DISC GOLF SCORECARD

| Date: | | Time: |
|---|---|---|
| Course: | | |
| Par: | | Distance: |
| Weather: | | Wind: |

| Hole | 1 | 2 | 3 | 4 | 5 | 6 | 7 | 8 | 9 | Out |
|---|---|---|---|---|---|---|---|---|---|---|
| Par | | | | | | | | | | |
| Distance | | | | | | | | | | |
| | | | | | | | | | | |
| | | | | | | | | | | |
| | | | | | | | | | | |
| | | | | | | | | | | |

| Hole | 10 | 11 | 12 | 13 | 14 | 15 | 16 | 17 | 18 | In | Total |
|---|---|---|---|---|---|---|---|---|---|---|---|
| Par | | | | | | | | | | | |
| Distance | | | | | | | | | | | |
| | | | | | | | | | | | |
| | | | | | | | | | | | |
| | | | | | | | | | | | |
| | | | | | | | | | | | |

Notes: _____
_____
_____
_____
_____

# DISC GOLF SCORECARD

| Date: | Time: |
|-------|-------|
| Course: | |
| Par: | Distance: |
| Weather: | Wind: |

| Hole | 1 | 2 | 3 | 4 | 5 | 6 | 7 | 8 | 9 | Out |
|------|---|---|---|---|---|---|---|---|---|-----|
| Par | | | | | | | | | | |
| Distance | | | | | | | | | | |
| | | | | | | | | | | |
| | | | | | | | | | | |
| | | | | | | | | | | |
| | | | | | | | | | | |

| Hole | 10 | 11 | 12 | 13 | 14 | 15 | 16 | 17 | 18 | In | Total |
|------|----|----|----|----|----|----|----|----|----|----|-------|
| Par | | | | | | | | | | | |
| Distance | | | | | | | | | | | |
| | | | | | | | | | | | |
| | | | | | | | | | | | |
| | | | | | | | | | | | |
| | | | | | | | | | | | |

Notes: _____

_____

_____

_____

_____

# DISC GOLF SCORECARD

| Date: | Time: |
|---|---|
| Course: | |
| Par: | Distance: |
| Weather: | Wind: |

| Hole | 1 | 2 | 3 | 4 | 5 | 6 | 7 | 8 | 9 | Out |
|---|---|---|---|---|---|---|---|---|---|---|
| Par | | | | | | | | | | |
| Distance | | | | | | | | | | |
| | | | | | | | | | | |
| | | | | | | | | | | |
| | | | | | | | | | | |
| | | | | | | | | | | |

| Hole | 10 | 11 | 12 | 13 | 14 | 15 | 16 | 17 | 18 | In | Total |
|---|---|---|---|---|---|---|---|---|---|---|---|
| Par | | | | | | | | | | | |
| Distance | | | | | | | | | | | |
| | | | | | | | | | | | |
| | | | | | | | | | | | |
| | | | | | | | | | | | |
| | | | | | | | | | | | |

Notes: _____

_____

_____

_____

_____

# DISC GOLF SCORECARD

| Date: | Time: |
|---|---|
| Course: | |
| Par: | Distance: |
| Weather: | Wind: |

| Hole | 1 | 2 | 3 | 4 | 5 | 6 | 7 | 8 | 9 | Out |
|---|---|---|---|---|---|---|---|---|---|---|
| Par | | | | | | | | | | |
| Distance | | | | | | | | | | |
| | | | | | | | | | | |
| | | | | | | | | | | |
| | | | | | | | | | | |
| | | | | | | | | | | |

| Hole | 10 | 11 | 12 | 13 | 14 | 15 | 16 | 17 | 18 | In | Total |
|---|---|---|---|---|---|---|---|---|---|---|---|
| Par | | | | | | | | | | | |
| Distance | | | | | | | | | | | |
| | | | | | | | | | | | |
| | | | | | | | | | | | |
| | | | | | | | | | | | |
| | | | | | | | | | | | |

Notes: _____

_____

_____

_____

_____

# DISC GOLF SCORECARD

| Date: | Time: |
|---|---|
| Course: | |
| Par: | Distance: |
| Weather: | Wind: |

| Hole | 1 | 2 | 3 | 4 | 5 | 6 | 7 | 8 | 9 | Out |
|---|---|---|---|---|---|---|---|---|---|---|
| Par | | | | | | | | | | |
| Distance | | | | | | | | | | |
| | | | | | | | | | | |
| | | | | | | | | | | |
| | | | | | | | | | | |
| | | | | | | | | | | |

| Hole | 10 | 11 | 12 | 13 | 14 | 15 | 16 | 17 | 18 | In | Total |
|---|---|---|---|---|---|---|---|---|---|---|---|
| Par | | | | | | | | | | | |
| Distance | | | | | | | | | | | |
| | | | | | | | | | | | |
| | | | | | | | | | | | |
| | | | | | | | | | | | |
| | | | | | | | | | | | |

Notes: _____
_____
_____
_____
_____

# DISC GOLF SCORECARD

| Date: | | Time: | |

| Course: |

| Par: | | Distance: | |

| Weather: | | Wind: | |

| Hole | 1 | 2 | 3 | 4 | 5 | 6 | 7 | 8 | 9 | Out |
|------|---|---|---|---|---|---|---|---|---|-----|
| Par | | | | | | | | | | |
| Distance | | | | | | | | | | |
| | | | | | | | | | | |
| | | | | | | | | | | |
| | | | | | | | | | | |
| | | | | | | | | | | |

| Hole | 10 | 11 | 12 | 13 | 14 | 15 | 16 | 17 | 18 | In | Total |
|------|----|----|----|----|----|----|----|----|----|----|-------|
| Par | | | | | | | | | | | |
| Distance | | | | | | | | | | | |
| | | | | | | | | | | | |
| | | | | | | | | | | | |
| | | | | | | | | | | | |
| | | | | | | | | | | | |

Notes: _____

_____

_____

_____

_____

# DISC GOLF SCORECARD

| Date: | Time: |
|---|---|
| Course: | |
| Par: | Distance: |
| Weather: | Wind: |

| Hole | 1 | 2 | 3 | 4 | 5 | 6 | 7 | 8 | 9 | Out |
|---|---|---|---|---|---|---|---|---|---|---|
| Par | | | | | | | | | | |
| Distance | | | | | | | | | | |
| | | | | | | | | | | |
| | | | | | | | | | | |
| | | | | | | | | | | |
| | | | | | | | | | | |

| Hole | 10 | 11 | 12 | 13 | 14 | 15 | 16 | 17 | 18 | In | Total |
|---|---|---|---|---|---|---|---|---|---|---|---|
| Par | | | | | | | | | | | |
| Distance | | | | | | | | | | | |
| | | | | | | | | | | | |
| | | | | | | | | | | | |
| | | | | | | | | | | | |
| | | | | | | | | | | | |

Notes: _____

_____

_____

_____

_____

# DISC GOLF SCORECARD

| Date: | | Time: | |
|---|---|---|---|
| Course: | | | |
| Par: | | Distance: | |
| Weather: | | Wind: | |

| Hole | 1 | 2 | 3 | 4 | 5 | 6 | 7 | 8 | 9 | Out |
|---|---|---|---|---|---|---|---|---|---|---|
| Par | | | | | | | | | | |
| Distance | | | | | | | | | | |
| | | | | | | | | | | |
| | | | | | | | | | | |
| | | | | | | | | | | |
| | | | | | | | | | | |

| Hole | 10 | 11 | 12 | 13 | 14 | 15 | 16 | 17 | 18 | In | Total |
|---|---|---|---|---|---|---|---|---|---|---|---|
| Par | | | | | | | | | | | |
| Distance | | | | | | | | | | | |
| | | | | | | | | | | | |
| | | | | | | | | | | | |
| | | | | | | | | | | | |
| | | | | | | | | | | | |

Notes: _____
_____
_____
_____
_____

Made in the USA
Monee, IL
15 July 2020